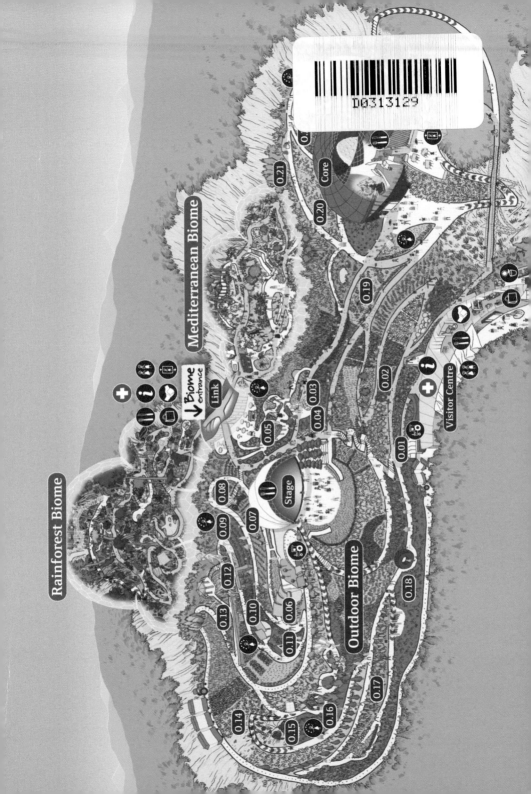

# Contents

Hello. We are delighted to welcome you to Eden.

This guide gives a flavour of all the different sorts of things we do.

For more information come and explore, visit the website, get involved in some of our projects and have a chat with our brilliant Eden team.

Have a great day!

**Planning your day**    4

## Your tour guide

**The Outdoor Biome**    6

**The Core**    16

**The Rainforest Biome**    20

**The Mediterranean Biome**    30

**What Eden is all about**    38

**What can we do?**    56

**Seasonal events**    58

**Where has the money come from?**    60

**Be involved**    61

**Biome maps**    64

# What Eden is all about – in a nutshell

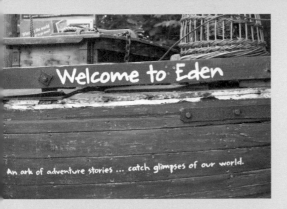

An ark of adventure stories ... catch glimpses of our world.

The Eden Project, an educational charity and social enterprise, creates gardens, exhibitions, events, experiences and projects that explore how people can work together and with nature to change things for the better. Project one: creating a global garden in a 50m-deep crater that was once a china clay pit as a symbol of regeneration.

This 35-acre living laboratory, which celebrates our relationship with plants and showcases the art of the possible, is an international visitor destination. Two vast Biomes, housing wild landscapes, crops and stories from the Rainforest and Mediterranean regions, act as a backdrop to our Outdoor Biome and the plants from our own climate. You can travel the world in a day, trek through the world's largest rainforest in captivity, meander through the Med, enjoy events and concerts, trace plants to plates and eat delicious foods all prepared with the planet in mind. Eden is a place to explore new ways of doing things in the 21st century.

There's much more to discover in the following pages – and, of course, on your journey round Eden today.

# Planning your day

## Stage

The home of our seasonal events programme: Freaky Nature, Eden Sessions, den building, summer circus, A Time of Gifts with ice skating. See the website.

🍴 **Great food in and around the Stage when there's an event on.**

## Outdoor Biome

Ten years ago this Biome (with the sky for a roof) was a barren landscape, with no soil and no plants. Take a look at it now; it celebrates our dependence on plants (for food, fuel, medicines and materials), presents our wild landscapes and explores their importance. It shows how people can work together, and with nature, to leave things better than they found them.

🍴 **Look out for food on the move – kids' boxes, pasties, baguettes…**

## Rainforest Biome

The largest rain-forest in captivity. Trek through the steamy jungle, get an amazing view from the Lookout 50m up, discover how rainforests keep us alive and how we can help do the same for them. Bananas? Coffee? Cashews? All here.

🍴 **Baobab juice bar open when possible.**

## Link

This grass-roofed building serves as the entrance to both covered Biomes. Loos, our little shop, membership and Annual Pass desks.

🍴 **Delicious food, cooked right in front of you in the Bakery – artisan bread, savoury treats, cakes, soups and stews. Join us round the kitchen table.**

## Mediterranean Biome

Sights, scents and stories from the Mediterranean, South Africa and California. Visit the wild landscapes and stroll through the world's kitchen gardens – wild vines, age-old olives, cork forests and much more.

🍴 Eden Med. Café for fresh, tasty Mediterranean food. Get in the holiday mood.

## Core

Home to exhibitions, art, schools programmes, and the 75-tonne Seed sculpture. Information on global challenges and possible solutions, and on our projects – and the world's largest nutcracker.

🍴 The Eden Deli – Baguettes, soups and salads.

## Lift and Bridge

join Core and Visitor Centre.

## Visitor Centre

The way in and out, tickets, membership and Annual Pass desks, our big shop, plant sales, ATM and loos.

🍴 The Eden Café. A pit stop on arrival or departure – sandwiches, soups, cakes, coffee...

## Land train

Every few minutes from Visitor Centre down to Stage Area and back up.

# The Outdoor Biome

# The Outdoor Biome

## View from the top

### Welcome to the Outdoor Biome 0.01

Stand on the viewing platform outside the Visitor Centre – or further down the path to the left at the Junction – to get an overview of the site. The exhibits below you tell stories of our dependence on the crops that grow in our own climate and show natural environments too. See the map on the inside front cover.

The entrance to both covered Biomes is in the grass-covered Link building between them.

## Zigzag area

### Flowerless garden 0.02

Journey through plant evolution, from the earliest mosses to the bryophytes, ferns and horsetails that grew in hot, steamy conditions over 350 million years ago, before the dinosaurs. They created coal as they rotted. Burning it releases the $CO_2$ they locked up and is heating up the planet again. More about climate change in the Core. Also look out for the first flowering plants, Magnolia and Drimys and the Wollemi pine, one of the world's rarest and oldest plants.

### WEEEman 0.03

Our waste giant is made from all the Waste Electrical and Electronic Equipment (about 3.3 tonnes) one person throws away in a lifetime. Designed by Paul Bonomini.

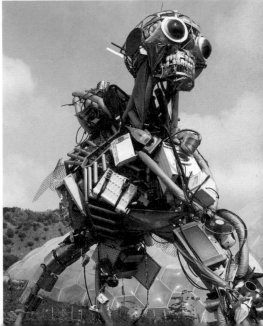

# Crops that feed the world  0.04

Three plant species – maize, wheat and rice – feed most of the world. They provide carbohydrates and some protein, and store well. Other major staples include potatoes, beans and bananas. Rapid world population growth led to wheat and rice breeding programmes in the 1960s and 70s to increase crop yields. This 'Green Revolution' staved off predicted large-scale starvation.

| **Wheat for...** | **Maize for...** | **Rice for...** |
|---|---|---|
| Bread | Corn on the cob | Rice (steamed, fried, etc) |
| Cakes, biscuits | Cornflakes | Rice Krispies |
| Pasta | Tortillas | Risotto |
| Wheat noodles | Animal food | Rice cakes |
| Animal food | Popcorn | Rice pudding |

Today's challenges include a growing population (nearly 7 billion, possibly growing to 10.5 billion by 2050); inequity in distribution; over-consumption and cheap food in many developed countries and hunger in many developing countries; a lack of reserves; rising oil prices; the food/fuel debate (see exhibit 0.12); land grabs; price hikes and climate change. Possible solutions include increasing yields and soil fertility, pest and disease resistance, biotechnology, agricultural biodiversity, new crops that can cope with the changing climate, trade justice, conflict resolution, poverty alleviation, good nutrition projects and education. On a personal level, thinking about what we eat and where it comes from, wasting less, eating less meat (60% of maize production is used as animal feed) and growing your own.

## The Garden of Senses 0.05

There are around 500,000 hectares of gardens in the UK (twice the area of nature reserves). Our own gardens represent a real, personal connection to nature, serving all sorts of purposes. We've represented a few here.

**A Sense of Memory** Inspired by memories of childhood Cornish holidays, this garden was created by Thomas Hoblyn, for the RHS Chelsea Flower Show 2011. Tim Smit saw the garden at the show and loved it; thanks to Tom and Homebase, who sponsored the garden, it was given a permanent home at Eden. People who have fond memories of particular plants have left their messages on the plant labels.

**A Sense of History** Garden flowers have their origins in wild places across the world. Favourites were bred to produce the garden varieties we are familiar with today. The dahlia originated in Central America; stems of its ancestors were once used as water pipes.

**A Sense of Place** This social garden has the environment close to its heart. Drought-resistant plants were chosen to avoid watering, and paths made from local materials to avoid air miles.

*Dahlia*

**A Sense of Play** Our play garden is made of willow and wood, helping to reconnect children with nature. Tip: push pieces of willow in and they take root, weave it into any shape you want. More tips on the website.

**A Sense of Taste** A productive garden half this size can provide a family of four with fresh veg all year round. And if you haven't much space just grow your favourites. Rocket only takes five to six weeks from sowing to eating.

**A Sense of Scents** Herbs, most of which don't need much water, are perfect for growing in pots. You know it makes scents.

**A Sense of Colour** A range of borders with themed colours: red, white and blue creating a stunning impact. Planting schemes are available from our plant shop and our website.

# Stage area

### The Hive in the orchard 0.06

Orchards: a place of relaxation and, in autumn, fast food (in a biodegradable wrapper). In the UK we produce only around 11% of our own fruit, but interest in health and local produce means that orchards are making a comeback. Try growing some tasty old varieties, start a community orchard near you, have an apple day. You can try some Cornish apple juice in our shop.

The Hive is a place where we show the Eden film or run workshops or sometimes even private events.

### Pollination 0.07

Plants can't move (much), so they reproduce by luring insects and other animals to take their pollen from flower to flower. Insect/flower relationships are often very specific. Over half our food plants worldwide depend on pollinators, so let's look after them.

Lavender, named from the Latin *lavare* ('to wash'), sedates and soothes. It is used in aromatherapy oils, perfumes, insect repellents and antiseptics. Bees' fondness for lavender flowers is often reflected in their honey.

### Cornish crops 0.08

Cornwall's mild climate means that it can supply the UK with early crops and quality foods year round. Eden food uses local produce wherever possible.

### Beer and brewing 0.09

Look out for beer ingredients (barley and hops), the hop stilt walker, the brewing kettle and the isinglass (tropical catfish swim bladder) used to clear beer, on our hop poles.

### Tea 0.10

Made from the young leaves of the tea bush, *Camellia sinensis*, tea grows in the subtropics, as well as the cool, moist, more mountainous tropics – and in Cornwall!

### Global gardens 0.11

Discover new veg to grow in your garden, from gardening communities with roots in Africa, Asia, Latin America, the Caribbean and Europe. The Heritage Seed Library (HSL) conserves rare varieties of vegetables. Become an HSL member and grow up to six rare varieties each year. **gardenorganic.org.uk/hsl**

## Crops for a material world 0.12

Plants can be grown for fibres, fuels and even plastics.

Industrial hemp provides food and health products, clothing, car components and building materials with a lower carbon footprint than concrete. Hemp grows well in the UK, needing few agro-chemicals (cotton uses around 25% of the world's pesticides). Legally we have to have a barrier round our hemp crop, so George Fairhurst designed us a hemp fence. He made our Metal Giant too. Give the rope a tug to see how strong plant fibres are.

Sunflowers provide high-quality oils for lubrication, plastic manufacture and biodiesel as well as food. Plant sugars and starch from maize and wheat make bioethanol for fuel and compostable plastic cutlery, carrier bags, nappies, etc. The UK's first bioethanol plant opened in 2010, creating a new market for wheat and mopping up the surplus we usually export. Plants grown for biofuels are having their carbon footprint scrutinised, and the food-versus-fuel debate means a search for alternative raw materials. Biomass to Liquids (BTL) factories will turn waste straw, wood waste, stalks, etc, into fuel, even biokerosene to power aircraft.

# West side

### Prairie 0.13

Looks great in full flower in August. The American prairies were partially created by man, using controlled burning to attract game (to young post-fire grass) and ease travelling. They once covered a quarter of the US. In some areas, up to 99% have been destroyed in the last 150 years. Work is underway to conserve these diverse grasslands and let the buffalo roam once more. Why conserve? Provision of ecosystem services (see the Core, page 19), climate control and potential future crops for starters. We manage our own prairie by burning in Feb/March, then the plants start to come through: Camassias, Liatris, Echinaceas ... Some public parks are now turning to prairie-style plantings: better for biodiversity, cheaper and easier to maintain than bedding.

*Echinacea*

### Plants for a changing climate 0.14

Our extreme gardeners explore adaptation and try new plants in tricky situations.

### Biomass fuels 0.15

David Kemp's 'Industrial Plant' sculpture and his 'Greenhouse of New Worlds' take a sideways look at fossil fuels, which currently provide around 85% of the world's energy. The developed world (16% of the world's population) uses 53% of this energy, while nearly half the world's people (mainly in developing countries) rely on wood, charcoal and dung, which have a low carbon footprint: the amount of $CO_2$ absorbed during their growth equals the amount emitted on burning. Willow, poplar and miscanthus are burnt for biomass in the UK. Other energy choices include wind and water power, algae as fuel, solar and nuclear power and geothermal, using heat from the earth.

## Myth and folklore  0.16

Stories keep plants alive in our memory, and our Pollinators bring you tales across the site. Pete Hill and Kate Munro created our willow Dream Chamber. Its classic seven-ring labyrinth is found worldwide. To sailors it was a good-luck token, ensuring safe return. It provided protection against wandering spirits who get lost in the curves (spirits can only travel in straight lines, allegedly).

## Wild Cornwall  0.17

Cornwall's biodiversity, its varied landscapes, habitats and wildlife, has been shaped by its climate, geology, geography and people. Heathlands are partly man-made; they started forming 6,000 to 3,500 years ago when woodland was cleared for hunting and agriculture, and need managing to prevent them reverting. Since 1800 Cornwall has lost over 90% of its lowland heath. Conservationists in Cornwall are helping to restore, protect and manage what is left. In Cornwall 75% of the land is farmed, though farming also provides rich habitats. Here, sculptors Peter Martin and Sarah Stewart-Smith have immortalised rare Cornish species in stone, and Chris Drury created the Cloud Chamber.

## Mining the earth: metals, minerals and energy  0.18

We're just as dependent on mining as we are on agriculture. But the environmental and social impact can be serious, both in the short and long term, and it is crucial to understand the industry's role and what constitutes good practice and responsible mining. Eden is a world-class example of the reclamation of an old mineral site. We have formed the Post Mining Alliance to work with industry and community groups to encourage and promote the regeneration of old mining sites (**postmining.org**). Turn the giant wheel to discover the story of the copper that made the Core roof. Climb into the mini tunnel to discover underground secrets.

13

# Core side

## Health 0.19

Half the herbs sold worldwide are wild-harvested, which, when done responsibly, can sustain environments and livelihoods. Herbs and pharmaceuticals (e.g. morphine derived from opium poppies) are also grown as crops. With 'pharming', crops are modified and used as biological factories to produce drugs.

*Pills from plants*

## Dyes 0.20

Woad and indigo give us blue, weld yellow and madder red. Indigo-dyed cloth comes out of the dye vat yellow and turns blue as it oxidises in the air.

## Paper 0.21

Plants growing here can be made into paper. Many natural habitats have been cleared and planted with Eucalyptus and *Pinus radiata* for paper-making. Agricultural residues containing cellulose, such as wheat and rice straw, can be used instead of wood pulp. World paper consumption is rocketing – so is recycling, luckily.

## The Spiral Garden 0.22

Making a school or community garden? Discover some low-cost ideas: willow spirals, rainbows of flowers, soft paths, textured plants, spooky plants and scented plants.

*Spiral Garden*

## Timber 0.23

The plant labels are made from the timber they describe. Wood is a carbon store and timber construction is on the rise. Good for wood.

## The Bluff 0.24

A place for picnics and play for children of all ages. Did you spot the secret paths through the tall grasses by the paper exhibit?

## Eden Project Adventure

For visitors with a sense of adventure: just on the edge of the pit we

have a Rock Wall and a Bouldering Wall.

NEW for 2012: Skywire — fly right across Eden on the longest zip wire in the UK. Opening summer 2012.

**For full details contact Eden box office on 01726 811972**
www.edenproject.com/adventure

## Outer estate

### Forest garden  0.25

On your way down to or back from the Visitor Centre, explore our new Forest Garden – full of native plants for food, shelter and medicines.

### Wild Chile  0.26

Behind Pineapple car park and between the totem poles take a trip to Chile and explore our forest of beautiful plants. Central Chile is under threat from logging, agriculture and replacement with non-native pine and eucalyptus for paper and wood chip. This 'Safe Site' contains and protects wild-collected material from the Valdivian forests of central Chile – a living example of ex-situ conservation. We are working with the Royal Botanic Garden, Edinburgh, and the International Conifer Conservation Programme.

*Embothrium*

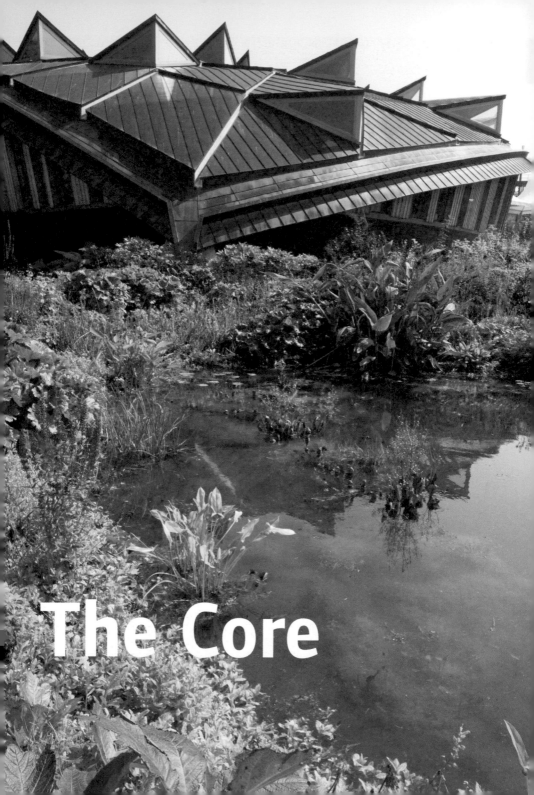

# The Core

# The Core

## Eden's education, arts and events hub

The Core isn't just a building, it's a metaphor. Its structure is based on a sunflower, which isn't a single flower but a collaborative project between hundreds of flowers which have united to create something better. Our projects, many of which are described in the Core, show how much can be achieved by working together.

The Seed, a 75-tonne sculpture carved from Cornish granite by Peter Randall Page, brings nature's blueprint into the heart of the building and plants a symbol of hope, to grow ideas for the 21st century. You can get up close on the ground floor.

# How the Core was built

**The brief** Fit for purpose, future-proof, made with responsibly sourced materials, energy efficient, with minimal waste. Grimshaws played another blinder, helped immeasurably by funding from the Millennium Commission, the South West Regional Development Agency and Cornwall's Objective One Programme.

**The structure** Double-curved glulam (glued laminated) timber beams, Swiss Forestry Stewardship Council endorsed.

**The form** Inspired by the growth blueprint of plants, opposing spirals based on Fibonacci's sequence: 0, 1, 1, 2, 3, 5, 8, 13, 21, 34 ... where every number is the sum of the previous two. The spirals on a pinecone, pineapple and sunflower, like our roof, usually represent two consecutive numbers in this sequence.

*The seed*

DO WE NEED ALL THIS STUFF?

**The roof** 40% of the world's copper is recycled. What about the other 60%, we wondered? Because of the way the market operates it can be almost impossible for the end user to ensure that metals are responsibly produced and sourced. We traced the supply chain of the copper for our roof from a single Rio Tinto mine, known for its high environmental and social standards, all the way to Eden. This unusual initiative has led to much more work on the minerals supply chain.

**Accessibility** The Core is on three floors, and built into the landscape so that each one is accessible from ground level.

**Floors** You'll find recycled wood, plant-based floorings (Marmoleum from flax, carpets from maize), and concrete from china-clay sand (low carbon footprint). The little green tiles are made from recycled Heineken bottles.

LUCKILY, THE AIR IS COMPOSED OF 21% OXYGEN

SO WE CAN BREATHE WITHOUT MASKS

# What's inside the Core?

**Ground floor** The huge glass ball of the Plant Engine represents the world's ecosystems (rainforests, oceans, grasslands, etc). It breathes life into the bell jars containing automata representing the 'ecosystem services' that keep us alive: controlling our climate, cleaning our air, recycling our water and waste, capturing our carbon and providing inspiration. Have a look at the cartoons round the bell jars to discover some of the amazing things the planet does for us – all for free –if we look after it.

Three challenges we impose on these systems – climate change, clean water provision, biodiversity loss – are explored in the little greenhouse, water tank and curiosity cabinet.

**Biodiversity** Life in all its richness and variety. Nature is important, we're part of it and it keeps us alive. Human impact is causing many species to disappear, and with them the patterns of life and the processes that our lives, economies and societies depend on. Biodiversity loss is an issue, because if it goes too far we will be among its first victims.

**First floor** This is where the classrooms for our schools programmes are (not often open to the public, sorry). You'll also find temporary exhibitions and films here.

**Second floor** Susan Derges created the windows around the solar terrace on this floor to symbolise the water cycle. On this floor you will also find delicious food in the Eden Deli.

IF WE HAD TO PAY FOR SERVICES PROVIDED BY ECOSYSTEMS WE MIGHT VALUE THEM MORE

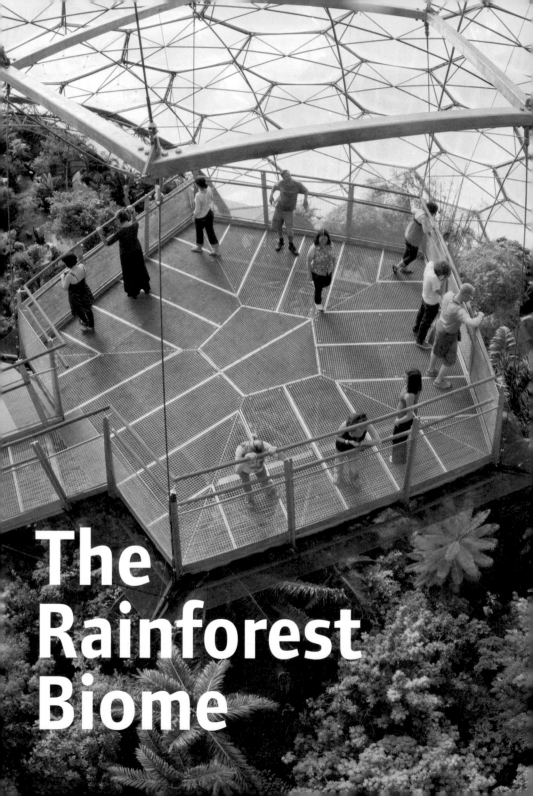

# The Rainforest Biome

# The Rainforest Biome

> 'Rainforest is the glue that holds the climate of our planet together. Lose the forest and it will have devastating consequences for all life on Earth.'
>
> Professor Sir Ghillean Prance, FRS

## Welcome to the Rainforest Biome R.01

The Humid Tropic Regions are located between the Tropics of Cancer and Capricorn, 23.5° N and S of the Equator. The average temperature is 25°C all year round (5°C variation), with over 90% humidity and 1,500mm (60") annual rainfall. We've recreated these conditions in our Biome (except we do the watering before you arrive!) and in the last 10 years have grown the largest rainforest in captivity. Why? The majestic rainforests that circle the globe are the planet's life-support system. We can't all go there; we decided to grow one here instead, so together we can explore their secrets, learn of the challenges and, most important, share ways of trying to save them.

On your Eden journey you can trek through four of the world's rainforests. The plants in each area may be different species but they have evolved to look similar to thrive in the climatic conditions. Millions of people live in and make their living from the rainforests; we bring you some of their stories. You'll notice half the Biome grows crops: chocolate, coffee, spices, rubber, medicines... Traditionally forest was felled to cultivate some of these things. We explore the search for balance: finding ways to grow crops to meet people's needs (supporting livelihoods as well providing consumer goods) whilst conserving the forest that keeps us all alive.

## How does the rainforest keep us alive?

Rainforests control the earth's climate, and help keep it cool. They absorb and store $CO_2$ in their wood. They also 'sweat', making huge white clouds, which reflect heat. It's 5°C cooler inside the Amazon than outside it. The rain they make waters crops across the world. They are also a huge store of biodiversity. Rainforests cover 5% of the earth's land mass and are home to half the world's plant and animal species. Some have been used to keep us fed, clothed and cured. Many have still to be studied. And the forests produce oxygen (but not as much as do the algae in the sea).

An area of primary forest the size of this Biome is cut down every 10 seconds. Don't panic (yet), rainforests can regrow. There are many things we can do too – read on! In our stories from the Rainforest area (R.11) you'll find further information and at set times meet one of our Pollination team who will share their stories.

# Explore the world's rainforests

## Tropical islands: conserving the land  R.02

Mangrove swamps protect the coast (e.g. against tsunamis), provide fuel, timber and a habitat for fish. Island habitats are home to many unusual, unique species. Climate change, invasive species, human settlement and tourism pose serious threats. Isolated island communities lack resources to conserve biodiversity, though conservation programmes offer hope: the rare Seychelles Coco-de-Mer, with huge seeds that look like giant bottoms, was over-harvested (as trophies and perceived aphrodisiacs). Now each seed is registered and protected. Ours (a gift from the Seychelles) germinated five years after planting: one of very few specimens in the UK, it grows slowly – a leaf a year. *Impatiens gordonii* (Seychelles) is threatened by loss of habitat. Eden, conservation bodies in the Seychelles and Reading University are propagating and conserving it.

## Malaysia: Orang dan Kebun (people and garden)  R.03

The contemporary Malaysian home garden provides food year-round. Herbs and flowers nearest the house, vegetables, fruit, and other useful trees further out. Winged beans replace our runner beans; both fertilise the soil. Pak choi, taro and rice replace cabbage, carrots and potatoes.

   The garden also provides building materials, medicines and produce to barter or sell at local markets. The miracle tree, *Moringa oleifera*, has edible leaves, beans, flowers and roots. Its seeds are used as water filters and its oils for watchmaking. To the left of the path is a rice paddy. In Asia 'rice is life', culturally and spiritually crucial to people's lives.

## West Africa: managing the land R.04

The totems, by West African sculptor El Anatsui, came from charred timbers recycled from a part of Falmouth docks which was destroyed by fire. They started their life as trees in West Africa.

On your right, penjaw: high forest is partially cleared and selected trees left to provide fruits, spices and medicines. Further round, the chop farm, where areas of forest are cleared, grows light-loving crops such as groundnuts, cassava, rice, millet and traditional African leafy vegetables alongside pawpaw, mango and bananas. Reverting to traditional crops in these areas rather than high-status Western crops helps provide a balanced diet and an income from local markets.

Our bantaba meeting place was created with help from the Ballabu Conservation Project, which hopes to create sustainable projects in and around 14 Gambian villages. We've a Gardens for Life project there too.

## Tropical South America: shamanic art and cassava production R.05

Take the steep and stepped high road past the waterfall for a great panoramic view and see the work of Peruvian shamanic artists Montes Shuna and Panduro Baneo, showing a spiritual connection between plants and people.

The flat low road takes you past the tallest tree in the Biome (the kapok).

The paths meet near a clearing where a hut shows the processing of cassava into tapioca. Cassava varieties contain prussic acid (hydrocyanide), which has to be removed before cooking!

### The Rainforest Lookout
You can get a bird's eye view from here (see picture on page 20) if you don't mind heights – it's 50m up.

**The Canopy Bubble** *This helium-filled Canopy Bubble is a genuine piece of research equipment used by scientists to study the rainforest canopy. Our green team use ours to study our canopy and to prune the parts that others cannot reach. It's also used in events, carried Ben Fogle and the Olympic torch, and occasionally we run competitions to let our visitors float into the treetops.*

*On the ground under the Bubble you'll spot our IKOS pod: canopy scientists' mobile living quarters – it sits high in the trees in the actual rainforest (… when our trees get a bit older and wider we'll do the same).*

## Welcome to crops and cultivation  R.06

Pass from the forest through the arch to find the plants that produce things we use: rubber, cocoa, chocolate, bananas … It's all a matter of balance between conserving the wild and cropping the land.

## Growing with the forest  R.07

'Slash and burn' is a common practice used in the tropics by desperate peasant farmers. Alley-cropping, in which the likes of cocoa, coffee, tea and pineapples are grown between rows of Inga trees, is a new alternative. This agro-forestry system is good for the trees and the crops, and transforms rural livelihoods. The trees provide shade, have delicious fruits (ice-cream bean) and can be coppiced (cut back) and used as a weed-supressing mulch which rots down to make fertile compost.
(NB: Not all legumes – pea and bean trees – have edible fruits; some are poisonous.)
The trees, like their relations peas and beans, have special bacteria living in their roots which make nitrogen fertilizer from the air. Win, win, win.

## Re-growing the forest  R.08

Rainforests can regrow. Archaeological evidence shows that over time 70% of the Amazon has been regenerated. Even so, it can be given a helping hand. Replanting pioneer trees quickly creates canopy cover, suppresses weeds, attracts animals that bring in seeds and nurtures timber tree species. Eden works on and with projects that help.

## Rubber  R.09

South American rubber trees, *Hevea brasiliensis*, provided rubber for boots and balls for centuries. In the 1700s Europeans used rubber for waterproof clothing and catheters. By the 20th century spiralling demand for car tyres stimulated the cultivated rubber industry in Asia. Synthetic rubber, from oil, came in when wars restricted supply. Rising oil prices and HIV-related demand for condoms and rubber gloves let natural rubber bounce back. Real rubber is also needed for high-spec uses such as aircraft tyres. Today, some rubber is sourced from designated areas of rainforest rather than plantations. We're now tapping the milky latex from our rubber trees right here.

## Cocoa and chocolate R.10

Cocoa originated in South America – you'll find its history on the cocoa wall. Today it is grown by around 2.5 million farmers, mainly on West African smallholdings. The

Want to know more about chocolate? Come and check out the Mayeaux Tapestry round the corner

UK chocolate industry supports schemes such as Fairtrade, improving livelihoods and protecting locals from global price fluctuations. Fairtrade also gives a premium that can be reinvested in business, social and environmental schemes. Scientists are crossing West African cocoa trees with their wild South American ancestors (we've some growing on the bottom path) to create disease-resistant trees – fewer chemicals and less planting on new land. So there's another reason to save the rainforest and protect its genes: it's where our chocolate comes from.

AZTECS CONQUERED

COCOA GOES TO SPAIN

**Did you know?** The scientific name for cocoa is *Theobroma,* meaning 'food of the gods'.

Our chocolate 'extra-ordinary' ice-cream is made with fairly traded fino de aroma Colombian cocoa. This is the top-notch type, quite rare, only 7% of the world's cocoa. It's said to be the tastiest in the world – judge for yourself!

*Ghanaian cocoa farmers from the Kuapa Kokoo Co-operative admiring Eden's cocoa crop*

## Palms R.12

Many palms are used in the tropics, for food, fuel, walls, thatch, ropes, boats, sago, sugar, cooking oil... However, one palm has become a global commodity. Oil palm produces 'vegetable oil', found in many processed foods and even in cleaning products and cosmetics. We no longer use palm oil in our Cornish pasties (even pasties sometimes contain palm oil). Global supply chases demand, and plantations march into the rainforest. In 2002 the Roundtable on Sustainable Palm Oil (RSPO) was established to address concerns. It is currently trialling a certification system: **sustainable-palmoil.org** Updates will be shown on site.

## Sugar R.13

Sugar is made from tropical sugar cane (and temperate sugar beet). In the 1300s we each used around a teaspoon a year. Today it's around 35kg, and stories of diabetes, obesity and poor teeth abound. Sugar cane is also used for ethanol production. According to the industry, this doesn't get caught in the food or fuel debate (unlike maize) and doesn't displace rainforest. Bagasse, the waste product, can be burnt to generate electricity. Seven million people are employed worldwide in the sugar industry, many in developing countries. Fairtrade and organic sugar are also on the up; all sugar used at Eden is Fairtrade.

## Tropical fruits R.14

**Bananas** Over 85% of the bananas grown in the tropics stay there, a staple diet for millions. Different varieties provide savoury or sweet dishes, juice, wine and beer. In our Biome, the banana conveyor and lower hut tell the story of the bananas that reach our shores: the Cavendish types from large plantations (such as those in Latin America, usually owned by large companies) or from smallholdings (such as those in the Caribbean, usually owned by local farmers). Organic and/or fairly traded bananas are available in shops; your wallet is your weapon. Panama disease has blighted Cavendish crops worldwide, so growers are trying new varieties – and so are we.

**Mango** For us a delicious treat, for some a promising export crop for developing countries and for others a vital famine food. The flesh makes medicines and wine; the nut oil cosmetics; and the wood, traditional drums and furniture.

**Baobab** We serve refreshing baobab juice when it's available. The baobab tree, from Africa, is called the tree of life. It can provide shelter, clothing and water as well as food. Our baobab fruit comes through PhytoTrade Africa and money raised helps support the harvesters in Southern Africa.

## Bamboo  R.15

Used by half the world's people, bamboo makes homes, furniture, food, fuel, music, medicine, scaffolding and suspension bridges. Its hollow tubes are strong but light. Within its tissues short, tough fibres sit in a resilient matrix: nature's fibreglass. Housings and Hazards, who bring people together to develop affordable, low-impact housing for vulnerable rural communities, helped make our house – Bam-Bams. Come in, sit and relax, maybe a game of chess?

## Coffee  R.16

Often under 10% of the retail price of this valuable product is earned by the exporting countries. Beans ripen at different times, so labour is intensive; mechanisation increases productivity but reduces quality. Our sustainably grown Eden-brand coffee uses Rainforest Alliance-certified beans, shade-grown under diverse trees, conserving biodiversity and helping deal with some of the effects of climate change (higher temperatures, drought).

## Nuts and spices  R.17

Today spices are cheap. In the past they were worth their weight in gold and shaped the world as we know it.

**Nutmeg** Though nutmeg was thought to cure the bubonic plague, it was along the spice route from Central Asia that the Black Death first travelled to Europe in the mid-1300s.

**Ginger** We're all familiar with root ginger, a globally traded spice, but this Zingiberaceae family has many relations: turmeric, cardamom, torch ginger, galangal … all part of daily life in the tropics. As well as flavour some are used in starch production, antiseptics and in cultural ceremonies. Some gingers are NTFPs (non-timber forest products). NTFPs can be harvested from the rainforest without harming the trees or environment. Good for plants, good for people. They'll be on the increase as they help make rainforests worth more alive than dead.

**Cashews** Why are cashews so expensive? Roasting, shelling and cleaning the nuts is laborious and the shells contain highly corrosive cashew-nut shell liquor (CNSL). Traditionally used to treat ringworm, CNSL is now sometimes used in heatproof enamels and brake pads.

## Secrets of the rainforest  R.18

Come and enjoy the beauty of these canopy plants.

## Challenges and solutions

Forests are cleared for agriculture, mining, development and timber. An area of primary forest the size of Eden's Rainforest Biome is destroyed every 10 seconds. 12–20% of carbon emissions (which contribute to climate change) come from deforestation. Over 100 species may be lost every day in the rainforests. Orang-utans' homes are destroyed when forests are felled to grow oil palm, found in nearly half the bestselling products in supermarkets.

## What to do?

Rainforests can re-grow or be replanted and managed sustainably for the future. To ensure our future survival we need to help the forests to survive.

- Understand how the forests keep us alive and share what you discover with others.
- Support charities and organisations working to save the forest.
- Shop for products which look after the forest (eg. FSC, Rainforest Alliance) and avoid products that don't (not just oil palm; forests are often felled to grow soya and meat).
- Write letters on rainforest issues to politicians at home and abroad.
- Volunteer for a rainforest charity (here or there).

## Eden's Canopy Walkway

Now our rainforest has grown up we're planning to put in a series of Canopy Walkways to explore the stories and secrets of the rainforest, including how they act as the planet's life-support system and what we can do to keep them growing. We've raised some funds, but still have a little way to go. Latest updates at **www.edenproject.com**

*The House in the Trees, Canopy Walkway*

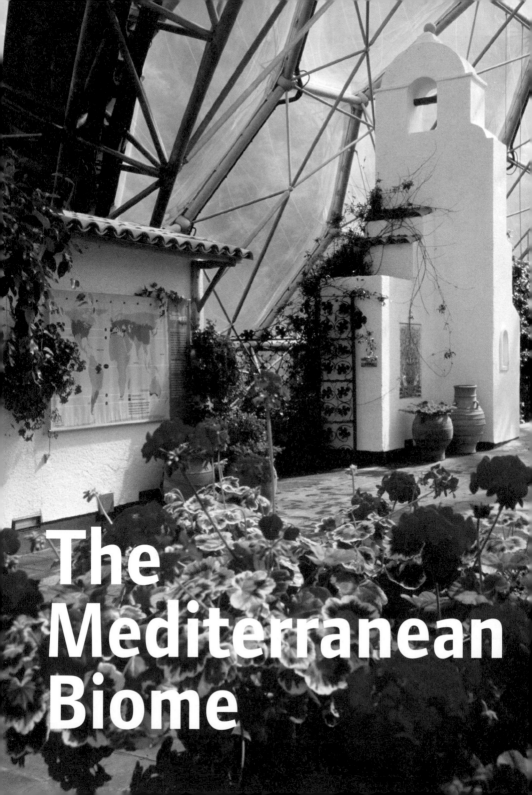

# The Mediterranean Biome

# The Mediterranean Biome

Salutare! Enter all – The Lands of the Warm Temperate Regions
Journey through:
The Mediterranean's Paradise
South Africa's Garden
California's Horn of Plenty
Born of Sister Fire and Brother Drought

Immerse yourself in Culture's Cradle
Taste history, olives, citrus and wines
In the world's kitchen gardens
Born of Water and Mankind

## Welcome to the Mediterranean Biome  M.01

Mediterranean-type climates with their hot, dry summers and cool, wet winters, are located 30–40°N or S latitude on the western sides of continents. They are within the Warm Temperate climate zone.

In this Biome we invite you to meander through the wild landscapes of the Mediterranean, South Africa and California. Wild? Through history many of these landscapes have been shaped by human cultures.

The native plants in all these regions have to cope with drought and poor, thin soils. Some have small, grey, hairy leaves, some make protective oils, some are spiny, evergreen and/or waxy. This may help to reduce water loss and make the plants less appetising to predators.

The plants are tough but their environments are fragile: intensive grazing erodes soils, imported plants threaten native species, land is developed and precious water is used to serve the needs of crops and people, many of whom are occasional visitors. Big pressure on small lands.

Crops? The addition of water and fertilisers to these sunny regions has created massive kitchen gardens for vegetables, vines, fruits and flowers. Take a look round. You'll find many familiar products come from these places: wine, olive oil, perfumes, lemonade.

On your journey, look out for Dionysus, the great bronze bull. He stands centre field, straddled between the wild and the cultivated lands. As he discovered (to his peril), it's all a matter of balance. It's in our gift to leave the world better than we found it.

## The Mediterranean Basin M.02

Through the gates to your left, a typical Mediterranean garden. Back on the main, lower route (no steps), the 'Liquid Gold' mosaic path created by Elaine Goodwin celebrates the tradition of olive oil as a symbol of life and divinity. Look for the subtle dove images – one for each Mediterranean nation.

The Mediterranean landscape is mainly man-made, cleared for crops over many thousands of years, including the olives and vines that helped shape this region's civilisation. The ancient terraced olive groves support more animal species than would a pine forest. Today many people leave their mountain farms seeking work on the coast, although city dwellers are beginning to return to smallholdings. Buying traditional foods and natural products, seeking out quality and taste, farm holidays: all can help conserve these fragile environments and communities.

Past the bell tower, the upper stepped route takes you through Maquis and Garrigue to the viewing point. The French underground movement in World War II was called the Maquis because they hid in this hilly landscape of prickly oak, juniper and broom, a habitat that contains unique plants, insects and reptiles, but can get overlooked, having no spectacular birds or mammals.

## South Africa M.03

The Cape Floral Kingdom has over 1,400 plant species which are rare or endangered. Fynbos, with around 7,000 species (5,000 unique to this area), covers 80% of this kingdom. *'Fain-boss'*, Afrikaans for 'fine bush', refers to the evergreen, fire-prone shrubs in this nutrient-poor soil. Plants include rush-like restioids, shrubby heathers and proteoids, with their stunning feather-like blooms. Formed millions of years ago from the ashes of drought-stressed forests, the Fynbos has been fire-managed for conservation since the 1960s; Protea seeds need exposure to smoke to germinate. The Fynbos is threatened by agricultural and urban development, uncontrolled fire and invasive alien tree species.

**Little Karoo**   In this semi-arid valley behind the southern coastal mountain range, the land bakes to 50°C in summer, freezes in winter and suffers severe droughts. Today much of the valley is irrigated for crops, but the surrounding hills house ice plants, aloes and types of daisy.

**Namaqualand**   This red desert, 250 miles north of Cape Town, blooms into a multi-coloured carpet after winter rain. Different species germinate in different years, depending on when the rains come, taking it in turns to share the scarce water. Descendants of these wild plants, pelargoniums and daisies, are garden favourites.

## California M.04

California has vast landscapes and a huge diversity of plants. Ceanothus and Californian poppies, familiar garden plants, grow wild here. The spiky chaparral, with its less familiar buck bush, toyon and scrub oak (the 'chaparro'), gave its name to

chaparreros, or 'chaps', worn by cowboys to protect their legs. Chaparral, grassland and the open oak forests were the results of thousands of years of controlled burning by Native Americans. California once had such a rich natural harvest that the indigenous people had no need to develop agriculture. Today water is so valuable that environmental activists take out court orders to make farmers leave minimum flows in rivers.

The state's high consumption brings social and environmental costs, putting it at the forefront of climate change. On the other hand, the region is also the birthplace of innovative new technology and home to some of today's most environmentally conscious people. The catalytic converter started life here and 2010 saw the first legislation to give polluting companies such as utilities and refineries financial incentives to emit fewer greenhouse gases.

33

## Welcome to crops and cultivation  M.05

Many of our crop exhibits are seasonal, so please expect changes from time to time. Producing crops in the Mediterranean regions is an intensive industry using fertiliser, water, sprays and often immigrant labour. Pressure is mounting to move to low-input, energy-efficient, diversified farming. Water is becoming increasingly scarce; many aquifers have more water extracted from them than they receive. Technologies are being developed to reduce usage and explore the re-use of clean seawater and waste water.

## Cork  M.06

Agriculture and conservation work hand in hand in the bio-diverse cork oak wood pastures. Cork bark is harvested and Iberian pigs, which feed on the acorns, help maintain the plant diversity and provide high-value ham. These trees, unlike others, don't die when their bark is cut off, so buying cork products supports these environments. Currently supply is outstripping demand. Organizations such as WWF, the RSPB and the Portuguese Cork Association work to conserve these wood pastures. Buying wine (and champagne!) with real corks helps, but cork has many other properties and uses. It can cope with extreme temperatures, so can be used as engine gaskets, for example. Maybe new industrial applications could help save these landscapes?

*The cork pigs by Heather Jansch (who also made the horse in the Visitor Centre)*

Sculpture by Heather Jansch

www.heatherjansch.com

## The Mediterranean orchard  M.07

Kiwis, peaches and loquats from China, almonds and apricots from Iran and Feijoa from Brazil have moved to the Mediterranean and California to soak up the sun and the water from the irrigation lines.

## Seasonal crops  M.08 / M.12

Depending on the time of year you'll find cut flowers, chillies, peppers, tobacco, grains, pulses (peas and beans) and a range of growing systems.

Chillies  There are dozens of varieties, from mild to unbearable. Chilli heat is measured in Scoville Heat Units, and the hottest variety found so far is rated at 1,382,118 SHU, whereas your basic super-market green chilli comes in at 1,500! Chillies and sweet peppers are easy to grow – you'll find seeds and plants in the Eden shop.

## Plants for perfume, clothes and flowers  M.09

Perfume  Feel free to touch and sniff. Try to describe the scent without referring to another smell. Tricky, isn't it? The scent of violets, a whiff of mint – scent goes straight to the seat of emotion and memory in the ancestral core of your brain. Plants use scent to attract pollinators and repel predators. Do we use it to signal, seduce or warn, like plants, or for sweet memory and comfort?

Clothes  Cotton is the world's biggest non-food crop, makes over a third of the world's textiles and traditionally uses high levels of water, fertiliser and pesticides. Organic and fairly traded cotton are on the increase.

Cut flowers  85% of our cut flowers are imported, causing environmental and social challenges but also potential for jobs and a step out of poverty. Check out the label. Seasonal blooms with low 'flower miles' mean you can say it with sustainable flowers! **edenproject.com/shop**

## Citrus  M.10

The citrus family is fond of breeding. Clementines are a cross between mandarins and bitter Seville oranges, and tangelos the offspring of tangerines and grapefruits. Citrus fruits provide vitamin C and nutraceuticals (more on these in the Core café). Citrus oils are used in flavourings, cleaning products, perfume, anti-bacterial agents, CFC substitutes and even fuel.

## Olives  M.13

Once olive oil provided light for lamps and anointed the brave. Now used mostly in the kitchen, it is thought to reduce cholesterol levels and deter heart disease. Production is up but the squeeze is on to reduce chemical inputs. Our older olive trees came from Sicily, having reached the end of their productive life. There is as much variation in taste and character in olive oil as there is in wine.

# Dionysus – a question of balance

*This potent nature god, here depicted as a bull, was associated with horticulture, fertility, wine, festivities, intoxication, illusion and also destruction. Dionysus started out with good intentions as the god of vegetation. However, things changed when he went from growing the vine to drinking its fermented juices ... party time! The land, like Dionysus, has changed. Here he stands, straddled between the ancient landscapes and the irrigated lands of intensive agriculture.*

*It's possible to go too far. It's possible to regain the balance. People can change things for the better.*

*Tim Shaw created this wild Bacchanal where dancing Maenads mirroring the shapes of the vines surround their god, Bacchus (aka Dionysus).*

## Grape vines  M.11

Grapes were one of the first cultivated fruits and today are the most widely planted fruit crop worldwide. Our long-term relationship stemmed from our ability to preserve them, by drying and far more consequential by turning them into an alcoholic drink. Jars of wine from Ancient Greece have even been found in modern Egypt.

From plant to plate: savour the flavour in the Eden Med café and watch your food growing around you

## The Mediterranean Café and vegetable garden  M.14

The classic Mediterranean diet is associated with good health and long life. The diet is based around:

- fresh vegetables (including greens, salads and legumes)
- fruits and herbs
- nuts and cereals
- olive oil (monounsaturated fat)
- a bit of fish, poultry and dairy (yogurt or cheese)
- small amounts of red meat (low intake of saturated fats)
- a little alcohol (usually wine with a meal)

However, is it just the food or is it also getting together with friends and family to relax and chat that does you good?

Artichokes Full of antioxidants, aid digestion, provide roughage and are used by some as a hangover cure. They are also said to lower bad cholesterol and to be good for the liver.

Tomatoes When tomatoes were first introduced, Europeans thought the bright fruits were poisonous so grew them as ornamentals and used their perfumed leaves to treat skin complaints. Now we know them as a good source of vitamins A, E, C and antioxidants.

# What Eden is all about

The Eden Project, established as one of the Landmark Millennium Projects to mark the year 2000 in the UK, is a visitor attraction featuring spectacular planting and spectacular architecture in a spectacular setting. (Chances are, if you're reading this, you already know that.) It is designed to give our visitors a great day out while demonstrating, in a serious yet playful way, how indispensible plants and people are to each other; how we all can adapt together to this challenging new world; and how even the most barren, worked-out china clay pit can be transformed into a place of beauty. The pit became a symbol of regeneration and our base to start to explore new ways of doing things. It's not just about conservation, it also involves repairing things we've messed up and re-inventing the world we have made. It's a demonstration, showing that by working together and with nature people can leave things better than they found them.

The Eden Project is also an educational charity. How does that work? While we try not to beat you over the head with it (we never forget that you're here for a day out, which is why the *New York Times* described our methods as 'education by stealth'), our principal business is education. At its simplest, if you leave here having discovered something about the cultivation and trade of bananas, say, or how building materials can be made out of hemp, that is within our remit. But we also carry out formal education programmes at all levels, from primary to tertiary, both here and all over the world. Your entrance fees and the money you spend during your visit go to support both the operation of our site and our public and formal education programmes and our projects. These projects, both on our doorstep and worldwide, explore new ways of living in the 21st century.

Eden is also a social enterprise, doing business to give the greatest possible benefit to the widest number of people and showing that improving the environment and livelihoods and building

> 'The future is ours to invent. Let's create a world we want to live in.'
>
> Dr Tony Kendle, Creative Director, Eden Project

stronger communities can work hand in hand. Since 2001 Eden's 13m+ visitors have helped us put well over a billion pounds into the regional economy through year-round trade with local suppliers and businesses. Over 80% of the money we spend on catering goes to Cornish suppliers; we work with local growers and companies to develop products for sale. Low food miles, seasonal and vegetarian dishes all help reduce greenhouse gas emissions. Fairtrade, organic and other certified products from further afield demonstrate that good trade is a vital part of sustainability.

# A symbol of regeneration

## The beginning of the story:

*'Around the late 1990s a small group of people gathered in pubs, hotels and offices to talk about an idea – to create a place like nothing anyone had ever seen before; a place that explored our place in nature, a place that demonstrated what could be done if people who wanted to make a difference got together. It was ridiculous to imagine it was possible and that hundreds of people trained to say no could be persuaded to say yes. But the greybeards had a brilliant plan: ask the youngsters to do it – they don't know it can't be done.'* Tim Smit, Eden

While Tim Smit was restoring the Lost Gardens of Heligan he realised that plants could be made far more interesting by weaving human stories around them, tales of adventure, emotion and derring-do. There was a big story to be told: plants that changed the world. A summer sunset on a china clay tip conjured thoughts of ancient civilizations in volcanic craters, and of putting the largest greenhouses in the world in a huge hole. Why not? We bought an exhausted, steep-sided clay pit 60 metres deep, the area of 35 football pitches, with no soil, 15 metres below the water table, and gave it life: a huge diversity of plants we use every day but often don't get to see, planted in soil made from 'waste' materials, watered by the rain, in giant conservatories and buildings that drew inspiration from nature.

> 'Never underestimate the power of a small group of people to change the world. In fact, it is the only way it ever has.'
>
> Margaret Mead

## Making it happen...

In 1994 Restormel, our local Borough Council at the time, took a leap of faith and put up the first £25,000, so giving the story a beginning.

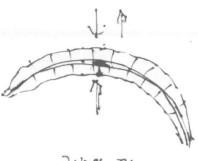

7·10·96  TH.

*The first Biome sketch, 1996, in the pub, on the proverbial napkin.*

A year on, Grimshaws the architects took the baton from Cornish architect Jonathan Ball (co-founder of the Project) and designed our fabulous buildings (at risk, though we paid them in the end!). The McAlpine Joint Venture worked for 18 months without payment or contract and then loaned Eden a significant sum only to be repaid if the Project was successful. This risk-sharing broke down the traditional barriers between designers and contractors and created a team dedicated to one vision. Why did they do this? Because they wanted to change something and because they wanted to say, 'I'm glad I did,' rather than, 'I wish I had.'

Sound simple? Not really. We were turned down by the Millennium Commission the first time we applied, and many left good jobs before we had raised a bean – or found a site. When our reworked bid secured £37.5m from the MC (huge thanks, MC), we had to match it. For the next 5 years a small team worked tirelessly (mainly in a shed) to turn the idea into a plan and then into reality. Finance Director Gay Coley (now joint CEO, Enterprise) came on board to raise the money, fledgling teams grew thousands of plants, mapped them on to the site, started planning the stories … We recruited a team to run the place and made sure that as well as having a good idea and a fabulous theatre we had the ability to operate it. The Visitor Centre opened in 2000 so the public could watch the construction and share the adventure. The whole site opened on 17 March 2001. For more, read Tim Smit's *Eden* and visit **edenproject.com**.

# Using plants as the canvas

Plants are our lifeblood: providing our crops, controlling the climate, making the very air we breathe. The natural world is our life-support system. At Eden we sow, grow and exhibit crop plants used for food, fuel, medicine, materials, beauty, music, sport, entertainment – to show and celebrate our dependence on the green things of life. We show our reliance on minerals and metals too; after all, we do live in an old mine. Stories across the site and in the exhibits section of this guide tell of land use, people and systems worldwide that keep us all alive and kicking.

You will find some of the world's wild places here too – including the largest rainforest in captivity. Forests, oceans, savannah, etc., provide 'ecosystem services', acting as air conditioners, water purifiers, waste recyclers, carbon capturers and climate controllers: all vital for our survival.

The point: to reconnect us all to our world, a reminder that we are part of it, to encourage us to care about it, because it's amazing and because it keeps us alive. Also a shot over our bows: what we do to nature we do to ourselves, we need to look after it in return. As Douglas Adams said: 'The world is big enough to look after itself. What we have to be concerned about is whether or not the world we live in will be capable of sustaining us in it.' Eden is not just about plants, it's about people. People working together, exploring what really matters, understanding the need to find a better balance between resource use (earning a living) and respecting and working with nature, understanding how to make a stand and what it is that tips us into action.

That's what 'Plant Takeaway' (known as 'Dead Cat') is all about. You can follow the adventures of Alan, Enid, Sniff the cat and Digger the dog in the children's guidebook.

*The*
***Plant Takeaway* – aka**
***Dead Cat, Visitor Centre.***
*Discover what happens when*
*the plants we use are*
*taken away.*

## Massive sandpit to global garden

To make the pit suited to people rather than mountain goats 17 metres was sliced off the top and put in the bottom. 1.8 million tonnes were shifted in 6 months. Dodgy slopes were shaved to a safe angle and terraces created. 2,000 rock anchors (some 11 metres long), stabilised the pit sides. A plant seed soup was sprayed on the slopes to knit the surface.

83,000 tonnes of soil was made. Minerals came from mine waste (sand from Imerys china clay and clay from WBB Devon Clays Ltd). In the Biomes, composted bark provided long-lived organic matter. The Rainforest Biome plants needed a rich organic soil that could hold water and nutrients, while the slower growers in the drier Mediterranean Biome used a sandier mix. A nutrient-free mix was used in South African Fynbos, where fertile soil is toxic to some native plants. Outdoors, we used composted domestic green wastes. Worms were added to help dig and fertilise.

## The Biomes: building the world's largest conservatories

Building 'lean-to greenhouses' on uneven surfaces is tricky. 'Bubbles' were used because they can settle on any shaped surface.

**Overall design** Two-layer, curved space frame, 'the hex-tri-hex', with an outer layer of hexagons (the largest 11 metres across), plus the odd pentagon, and an inner layer of hexagons and triangles bolted together. The steelwork weighs only slightly more than the air contained by the Biomes. They are more likely to blow away than down, so are tied into the foundations with ground anchors (giant tent pegs).

**Transparent foil 'windows'** Ethylenetetrafluoroethylenecopolymer (ETFE): three layers, inflated 2-metre-deep pillows, lifespan over 25 years, transmit UV light, non-stick, self-cleaning. They weigh less than 1% of the equivalent area of glass, but can take the weight of a car. We got into the *Guinness Book of Records* for using the most scaffolding, 230 miles of it – sorry to anyone who was needing some that year.

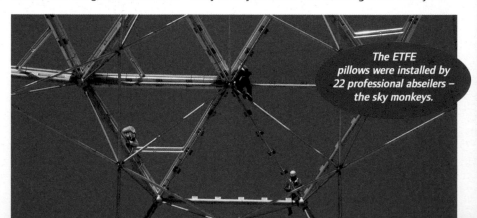

*The ETFE pillows were installed by 22 professional abseilers – the sky monkeys.*

# Extreme gardening

Our Green Team often plant on near-vertical banks; have planted millions of plants of around 5,000 types, plant over half a million bulbs every autumn; plant around 60,000 new plants annually; start at 7.30 every day to prune and water before you arrive; do 50 hours weeding a week in the summer; remove about 25m³ of green waste from the site every week; recycle this material to make over 120 tonnes of compost a year.

**Plants** Many are grown from seed in our nursery, some come from botanic gardens, research stations and supporters, mostly in Europe and the UK. We keep a record of every plant on site. Pollination: some plants are insect-pollinated, some wind-pollinated, some paintbrush-pollinated! We do this when we need the flowers to produce seeds.

**Pruning** Rainforest trees are pruned by abseilers, from a cherry picker and a Canopy Balloon (page 24).

**Pest and disease control** Our rigorous healthcare programme starts with isolation houses at Eden's nursery to catch problems before they reach the site. On site our integrated pest management system uses cultural methods (removal of infested plant parts), 'soft' chemicals (soaps and oils) and biological control (bugs that eat

bugs). Spot the little bamboo pots on pulley systems that give the bugs a ride to the treetops. We also have some birds and lizards in the Biomes which eat their fill of pests. Our UV lightboxes catch pests and monitor their numbers.

**Climate** In the covered Biomes it is monitored and controlled automatically. The main heating source is the sun; the back wall acts as a heat bank, releasing heat at night. Triple-'glazed' windows provide insulation, while air-handling units cool on hot days and heat on cool ones.

**Rainforest Biome** Misters create 90% humidity, irrigation comes from ground-level pipes.

**Mediterranean Biome** Drier; even in cooler periods the vents often open to reduce humidity and fungal problems.

# The way we work

Since opening in 2000 we've developed exhibitions, events, workshops, courses, education programmes (for all), concerts, sustainable buildings, efficient operating, energy and waste systems and grown our team to over 500.

Eden is a project, a living laboratory exploring new ways of doing things. The way we operate and the projects we run (more on these later) all test ways of living in the decades to come. We take people, the planet and profits with a purpose into account ('the triple bottom line' as it is often called). This begins with building an awareness of what we dare not lose and exploring what we need to work with to help create a viable society in the 21st century: massive social and environmental change, carbon reduction, energy security, food security, conservation, building communities that can cope.

## People

Eden has grown from 5 staff to over 500, plus 300 volunteers. Teams report to the Board, who report to the Trust, who ensure the operation meets its charitable aims. Art, science, horticulture, education, management, retail, catering, philosophy, economics, design, construction, publishing, research, housekeeping, stewarding, guiding, fundraising, storytelling, marketing, media – between them the teams cover all these bases and more. We work with others whenever we can to discover new approaches and to share what we have learnt.

We explore creative approaches to physical access and information sharing to make our work accessible to all. **www.sensorytrust.org.uk**

# We love stories

Story is a powerful means of captivating, providing insight, testing moral choices, painting possible futures, challenging and holding a mirror up in a way that is acceptable – personal and impersonal at the same time. Unless a culture has strong stories it loses its direction. Eden aspires to be a place where the stories of our future are created and told – the *Aesop's Fables* of the 21st century. Look out for our Pollinators (Eden's storytellers and guides), who will share their stories with you.

## Learning programmes

Our schools programme hosts over 45,000 young people a year from the UK and a further 10,000 from overseas. We aim to help provide context, purpose and meaning. You may spot young explorers in 'Don't Forget your Leech Socks' trying their survival skills in the rainforest, reconnecting with science on the ultimate field trip. We also welcome over 10,000 further and higher education students annually, covering a wide range of subjects including continuing professional development for teachers. This year our leisure learning courses also kick in. See the website for details.

*Storytelling*

49

# The way we work

## Planet

We're committed to reducing our carbon footprint, using resources efficiently, generating our own renewable resources and being self-sufficient in soil, water and energy where possible. Our tens of thousands of plants sequester carbon every day. We offset all our direct emissions, electricity and business travel through ClimateCare and operate a green travel plan. You can get involved too: see our website **edenproject.com.**

## Energy efficiency
The Biomes' hexagons copy nature's honeycombs: maximum strength, minimum materials. All our buildings set high standards for good building design and process, and demonstrate the worth of natural materials and structures. Since 2008 we've reduced our emissions from gas use by 25%, and electricity by 23%, despite opening a new café in St Austell and baking all our own bread. New control systems, boilers, lighting, etc (thanks partly to an interest-free loan from the Carbon Trust), should see a 25% reduction in $CO_2$ emissions by 2013.

**Waste neutral** We reduce, re use and recycle our waste wherever possible (currently recycling 19 different waste streams) and we reinvest by purchasing items that are made from recycled materials. Since 2005 our in-vessel composter has turned 160 tonnes of food waste and 34 tonnes of green and cardboard waste into 110 tonnes of plant compost for use on-site.

**Cleaner technologies** Photovoltaic panels on the Core roof and a small wind turbine generate clean electricity. Nearly half our water needs – averaging 20,000 bathfuls a day – are provided from grey water harvested on site by a subterranean drainage system. We use it to irrigate our plants and flush our loos, while rainwater that falls on the Biomes is used to create the mist inside the Rainforest Biome.

> 'You never change things by fighting the existing reality. To change something, build a new model that makes the existing model obsolete.'  R. Buckminster Fuller (1895–1983), architect, designer, visionary

# Project: Geothermal

With EGS Energy, we've got planning permission for a deep geothermal plant to supply us with zero-emission heat and power, and export the excess electricity, enough for around 3,500 households. This new technology, if rolled out, has the potential to supply as much as 20% of the UK's electricity and all of its heating! More on this and our energy policy and action plan at **edenproject.com/energy**.

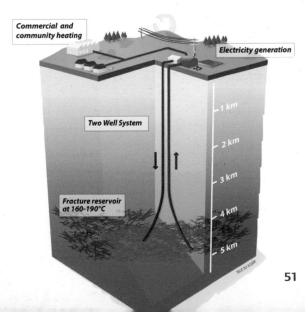

Commercial and community heating

Electricity generation

1 km

Two Well System

2 km

3 km

Fracture reservoir at 160-190°C

4 km

5 km

Not to scale

On the journey of building and operating Eden we discovered, explored and shared what people needed to find within themselves to achieve something they really believed in, often working against the odds. At Eden, hope was the motivator, a genuine belief that the future could be faced with optimism. Also trust, in getting enough people to buy into one vision, and trust in each other to realise it. Other ingredients included huge dollops of ambition, courage, energy, collaboration, determination, can-do attitude, passion, a touch of madness and an underlying vital purpose.

An inherent part of our story is to look at challenges the world faces/ that we face, the realisation that it's not all rosy, that we have to take responsibility and, most importantly, we need to approach this with hope. Eden was initially a response to our disconnection with nature. Today it is also a provocation to do things differently. We wondered if the lessons we'd learnt could be applied in other situations.

The result: we now work, with many others who we've met along the way, on projects for climate (education, reducing carbon and coping with change), projects for places (improving environments), and projects for people (harnessing/cultivating talents and skills, building stronger communities). Projects that explore what people can achieve when they work together and with nature.

## Projects for climate

We explore what can be done, including education around climate change, mitigation (reducing its effects) and adaptation (changing how we live to respond to it). Working with a range of partners, a recent climate project, Clear about Carbon, creates exhibits, workshops and helps businesses understand more about the low-carbon economy and how they can work towards it. **clearaboutcarbon.com** (don't miss the stunning animation).

## Projects for places

The first one: on our doorstep, regenerating this pit. Worldwide we work on a whole range of regeneration initiatives, including those in tropical islands and rainforests (these will gain momentum as we build our Walkway, see page 29).

### Gardens for Life – an Eden Project
Crossing communities, cultures and countries, Gardens for Life is a network of schools that explores the world through gardening and growing food. Find out more in the blue allotment shed at Eden and at **edenproject.com/gardens-for-life.**

# Projects for people

## Building stronger communities

**The Big Lunch** encourages people across the UK and beyond to get together with their neighbours for a few hours of community, friendship and fun. The Eden Project started the Big Lunch because it believes that we are better equipped to tackle challenges when we face them together. **www.thebiglunch.com**

In 2012 the Big Jubilee Lunch formed part of the central weekend of celebrations to celebrate Her Majesty the Queen's Diamond Jubilee. An estimated 6 million people across the UK as well as people in communities in 70 countries across the world sat down to lunch together during the holiday weekend. In 2013 the Big Lunch will be on Sunday June 2.

# Projects for people

## Harnessing and cultivating talents and skills

Projects with communities, businesses, schools, colleges, the vulnerable and excluded.

**Green Foundation** offers a range of professional development programmes that aim to inspire and empower businesses to innovate, collaborate and lead positive change within and beyond their organisations. Our programme touches on everything from reducing inefficiencies to introducing sustainable operations, from communicating with staff to creating action plans. **greenfoundation.org.uk**

**How2** is the beginning of Eden's second chapter. Within its walls it will provide an environment where students from diverse backgrounds can learn practical skills, work with technology, develop creativity and innovation. The setting of the wider Eden Project estate will be put into service to give the students creative challenges, inspiration and real projects to work on that embody a high level of belief and ambition. How2 is built on the three pillars of Creativity, Technology and Making. It is a place where skills are taught, but also where aspiration is fostered. A vibrant mix of creative approaches to practical training will be linked to tangible results - demonstrations of practical change that show how the world is still ours to make.

Our journey continues, working with others, exploring new ways of doing things, using creative solutions, new models, and new rules that are fit for the 21st century: in education, in business and in communities.

# What can we do?

There's no shortage of top tips for a greener life: fitting energy-saving light-bulbs and so on. Useful? Yes and no.

They can trivialise the issues; saving the world isn't a matter of what goes in your basket, and it takes the heat off the big guys. But if we had to write our own Ten Top Tips (eleven, actually!), they'd go like this:

**3. Learn about your life** Is having 'stuff' bad? Not always: trade is not the same as consumption and can support livelihoods. Understand what sustains you and what you need to care about. Learning new talents and skills can help you get there.

**1. Do stuff** Don't waste it, turn it off, turn it down, do it less, do it local, do it yourself, recycle, swap, repair, share.

**4. Increase your reach** There's only so much you can do on your own. Try working with or through other organisations. Also don't forget that your wallet is your weapon. Make buying choices that help good things happen – worldwide.

**2. Be hopeful** Hope isn't just about crossing your fingers. Without it we could get cynical and frozen in despair. Hope is the fuel – but it only works if you do something.

**5. Be angry at the things you can't change** … but think about who can change them. Demand that governments, companies and big organisations change with us and give us real choices.

**6. Imagine different things** The 21st century will be a time of transformation. Meet different people, explore different things, read different books, try out new ideas.

**7. Give gifts and give thanks** Understand why we need each other. This is a time to support each other, to work together and build communities.

**8. Get out more** People can't care about what they don't understand and don't have some sense of connection to. So we need to get out and down in that dirt lest we forget how it keeps us alive. Play together, learn, explore and have adventures.

## 9. Forgive yourself (and others)

Sustainable development will be a territory for endless exploration. Learn from mistakes. We make mistakes because we act, strive and aim high – and that is what makes us human.

**10. Have fun** 'Living a sustainable life' isn't all about 'don't do this' sucking the joy out of living. Where is the adventure in that? There are worlds of possibility out there. Rich cultures, rich experiences, music, laughter, fun and just enjoying life more – foundations for a better future!

**11. Be the change you wish to see in the world** Gandhi's saying sounds like something from a hippie poster, but actually it was one of the greatest social insights of the 20th century. So, do everything positive you can, not because a list has told you to but because it's who you want to be.

# Seasonal events programme

You'll find a different Eden every time you visit. Here's a flavour. For the latest programme visit **edenproject.com/whats-on**

## Spring into life

**Eden's Chocolate Festival** with chocolate, chocolate – and more chocolate!.

**Freaky Nature:** Discover reality that's so bizarre you couldn't make it up!

## Wild summer days

**Dens, music, fire, barbecues, performance** … playful outdoor activities for all.

## Autumn fare

**Harvest at Eden** – The world's bounty, celebrate it, preserve it, eat and drink it.

**Halloweden** – All things spooky and icy too.

*Den building*

## Winter wonderland

Our **Time of Gifts** winter festival: ice skating, music, processions, workshops and markets. A time to give thanks for the things we give each other and the natural resources that nurture us.

*Time of Gifts*

# Ticketed events

**Eden Sessions** (**edensessions.com** for bands and full details)

Circus and other ticketed events (**edenproject.com**).

**Party time:** Some for adults, some for all and some just for the kids (**edenproject.com**).

*NoFit State Circus*

# Leisure learning

New this year: Gardening courses and experience days, including 'Be a Gardener for the Day' and 'Canopy Balloon Experience', plus a range of other courses coming soon. Contact the **boxoffice@edenproject.com** or ring 01726 811972 for details or to register interest.

*Party time*

# Where has the money come from?

The Millennium Commission weighed in with £37.5m of lottery funding to single Eden out as the 'landmark' project of the far South West, and their subsequent contributions brought the total to just over £56m. We hope we've delivered for them and for anyone who ever bought a lottery ticket. Other major sources of funding included the EU and Southwest Regional Development Agency (some £50m between them) and £20m of commercial loans. The balance was made up of other loans and some funds generated by Eden itself and reinvested back into the Project.

Maintaining a strong and diverse financial base is crucial to preserving the Eden Trust's independence and credibility. A full list of all our funders to date can be found at **edenproject.com/thankyous**. Thank you.

## How much?

| | £m |
|---|---|
| Buying a large and unusual site, car parks, roads and paths | 16 |
| Reshaping the ground to make it safe, dry and useful | 8 |
| A couple of decent greenhouses | 25 |
| 40 acres of plants ... some tall | 3 |
| 83,000 tonnes of manufactured soil to grow them in | 2 |
| A nursery to practise in and grow some unusual plants | 1 |
| Buildings for you and our team – fully equipped | 22 |
| Services to keep it all running | 7 |
| Paying the team up to opening | 3 |
| Exhibits to entertain you, walkways to keep you dry, a lift, a bridge | 12 |
| Advice on the things we couldn't do ourselves | 12 |
| Investments in our future like the Foundation building | 9 |
| A spectacular home for education – The Core | 16 |
| Warehouse, gatehouse, waste compound, Arena | 4 |
| **Dreams cost money** | **Total 140** |

# Be involved

Eden is a charity and our work and successes are only possible thanks to the generosity of our donors, supporters and volunteers. **edenproject.com/support**

## You can support our work in many ways

**Visit us** You're helping just by being here – all the profits from your visit go to the Eden Trust.

**Gift Aid your admission fee** This allows us to claim 28p back from the taxman on every pound you give.

**Become an Eden Friend** Eden Friends enjoy free entry to Eden, get exclusive access to our horticulture team, and play a vital role in supporting our charitable work.

For full details go to:

- **edenproject.com/friends**
- the Friends information points (see site maps)
- 01726 811932
- **friends@edenproject.com**

**Make a donation** edenproject.com/donations
The money we raise goes towards our work on public and formal education, research, conservation and sustainable futures.

**Volunteer** edenproject.com/volunteer
Can you spare at least 6 hours a fortnight? Feel good, learn things, meet people – what's not to love? An ideal way to become involved in the daily work of the Project.

## Register for our newsletter edenproject.com/newsletter

## Useful numbers

General enquiries: 01726 811911 Box office: 01726 811972
Group bookings: 01726 811903 School bookings: 01726 811913

The Eden Project, Bodelva, St Austell, Cornwall PL24 2SG
The Eden Project is a registered charity no. 1093070

## Contact us edenproject.com/contact-us

First published 2001 by Eden Project Books, a division of Transworld Publishers
Twelfth revised edition 2012

Text and design © the Eden Project/Transworld Publishers 2012

Text by Dr Jo Elworthy with assistance from the Eden team

Transworld Publishers, 61–63 Uxbridge Road, London W5 5SA,
a division of the Random House Group Ltd

**booksattransworld.co.uk/eden**

ISBN 9781905811854

Editor: Mike Petty  Design: Charlie Webster  Printed in Great Britain

MIX
Paper from
responsible sources
FSC™ C023561
FSC www.fsc.org

The Eden Project is owned by the Eden Trust, registered charity no. 1093070
and all monies raised go to further the charitable objectives.

Eden Project, Bodelva, St Austell, Cornwall PL24 2SG
T: +44 (0)1726 811911  F: +44 (0)1726 811912

**edenproject.com**

This project is
part-financed by
the European Union
Working with Objective One

One
The Objective One Partnership
for Cornwall & the Isles of Scilly

South West *of* England
Regional Development Agency

Supported by
**The National Lottery®**
through the Millennium Commission

M
Millennium Commission